Why Me, Lord?

Phil Fethers has had a strange life. Every time he thinks things are finally straightening around to normal, the bottom falls out.

There has to be a reason. He's determined to find it.

Why Me, Lord?
© 2013 by C. D. Moulton

all rights reserved: no part of this publication may be reproduced or transmitted in any form or by any means, electronic or mechanical, including photocopy, recording, or any information retrieval system, without permission in writing from the copyright holder/publisher, except in the case of brief quotations embodied in critical articles or reviews.

This is a work of fiction. Any resemblances to actual persons (except me) or events is purely incidental.

Contents

Birthday 30	pg. 1
Strange Visitor	pg. 11
Stroke of Luck	pg. 19
Another Ho-hum Day	pg. 35
Tomorrow's Petty Pace	pg. 46
What Next, Lord?	pg. 51
A New Assignment	pg. 57
One Year Later	pg. 65

About the author

CD Moulton has traveled extensively over much of the world both in the music business, where he was a rock guitarist, songwriter and arranger and in an import/export business. He has been everything from a bar owner to auto salvage (junkyard) manager, longshoreman to high steel worker, orchid grower to landscaper, tropical fish farmer to commercial fisherman. He started writing books in 1983 and has published more than 350 books as of January 1, 2023. His most popular books to date are about research with orchids, though much of his science fiction and fantasy work has proven popular. He wrote the CD Grimes, PI series, and the Det. Nick Storie series, Clint Faraday series, and many other works.

He now resides in Gualaca, Chiriqui, Panamá, where he writes books, plays music with friends, does research with orchids and medicinal plants. He has lately become involved in fighting for the rights of the indigenous people, who are among his closest friends, and in fighting the extreme corruption in the courts and police in Panamá.

He offers the free e-book, *Fading Paradise*, that explains what he has been through because of the corruption.

CD is the discoverer of the Chadam Protocol for curing cancer.

Facebook page Ambrosia peruviana for cancer.

<u>*Birthday 30*</u>

Phil Fethers woke up early with a headache and his right foot hurt.

He groaned. Not another day like yesterday! It simply couldn't go on and on and on and on. It was his birthday, and he woke up to dred, not joy.

Hell, not even contentment.

Phillip James Fethers, 30, as of today.

Why the hell didn't they name him Tarand Fethers? It would fit his life!

He swung his leg to the bedside. Charlie horse! He screamed a short agonized, "Gheee!" and grabbed for his foot. Pull back on the toes. The charlie horse lessesed. He worked the knee a bit, sighed, swore, and stood. Today would be Hell plus. He should stay in bed.

The way he had to piss, even that would lead to disaster.

He went to the bathroom. This was, at least, something he could get relief from. He took a long piss, stepped back, flushed the toilet – which was clogged, somehow. The water came over the rim and was running onto the floor. The tank float didn't cut off the fill. He dove for the cut-off valve, banging his head on the sink The flow stopped, but he had a mess.

What's new? He went to the cabinet for the mop. The detergent was turned over and had run onto the floor. He stared at it a few seconds, shook his head, took the mop to dry the bathroom floor, went back, put the mop in the cabinet and took out the plunger.

He didn't ask why the toilet was clogged. There was no answer. He had put nothing in it that could clog, but this kind of thing happened much to frequently to him for him to waste time wondering about it.

He got the toilet to working. He had the water squirt all over him when he used the plunger. He stepped into the shower to rinse off. There was a sudden knot in the arch of his foot. He slipped, but managed to grab the shower curtain before he fell onto the tile.

That pulled part of the rings off the rod, of course.

The phone rang. Why?

He was in the shower. Of course it rang. It always did.

Fuck it! He went into the hall wet to answer the phone. It quit ringing just as he got to it. Naturally.

He went back to the bathroom and towelled off.

The phone rang again. He answered it this time. Jennie Wright. Pain in the ass needy girl who had latched onto him tighter than a leech. He didn't want to hurt her. He didn't want to hurt anyone, so he ended up being hurt. Every time.

There was a party at her place. Seven thirty. It was for him. Be there.

He went to the kitchen, put on the coffee, and got out the bacon, eggs, and makings of an omelet – which would turn into scrambled eggs with vegetables and bacon bits before he was done. He never could turn an omelet.

He dumped the mix into the hot skillet. A bit of hot oil spattered on him. A couple of burn blisters. Small, for a change.

There was a loud knock on the front door. Crap! It was too early for anyone he knew to be here!

He turned the stove off and went to the door. Four Jehova's Witnesses or Seventh Day Adventists or something were there. Two men and two women. He opened the door. They were shocked. The women squealed and ran down the walk. The men stared a second, then said they didn't need any perverts in their church and marched off.

Shit! He forgot he got out of the shower and went directly to the kitchen. He didn't put anything on.

Maybe that would work out alright. That bunch definitely wouldn't return!

Wrong! He went back to the kitchen and started the omelet to cooking again. The coffee was ready. He poured a cup and put in a sugar cube, stirred it, and took a sip.

What now? It tasted very strange!

Shit! He'd put a boullion cube with garlic in it, not sugar!

There was a knock on the door. He grabbed the towel and wrapped it around him, this time.

One of the religious nuts was there. He said they had possibly over-reacted when he came to the door nude. Perhaps he didn't dress in his own home, which was a bit strange, but not illegal. The way the guy stared, it was obvious he hoped Phil would still be nude.

"You do believe in God, in Jesus Christ?" he intoned.

"In *a* God, yes. In Christ, no. I used to believe, but I know very well that God is a vicious sadistic monster. It's the only explanation for my life. This could not be happening without malicious direction."

"Er, um! You could ... I will leave some things with you. You will see that your life can become one of joy and salvation, not a sordid search for meaningless things and money and sex."

"I get by okay. I'm not after money or things. You, of course, would appreciate it if I could see a way to donate a few dollars to your cause to save the world from itself whether it wanted to be saved or not."

"Money and things, but sex? You would continue to seek physical pleasures, if not the material things?"

"Sure! Why not? No, I'm not interested in a little diversion right about now. It's too early in a miserable morning."

"Er, um! I, er, that is. Perhaps another time. I will leave a few things for you to read."

"Uh-huh. They go right to the circular file. I've read it all. It's bullshit. I really do have things to do. Excuse me if I don't care to hear your particular line that is the only true way. It's the same one hundreds of other cults claim. Have a nice day." He closed the door in the idiot's face.

What was that smell?

He hadn't turned the stove off this time. The omelet was a coating of charcoal on the skillet.

He swore tiredly, cleaned the skillet, and saw that he'd used the last two eggs.

No sweat! He had a bunch of chickens wandering around the yard all the time. Two had nests by the garage. He went out and got six eggs from the two nests and went back inside.

He put four of the eggs in the 'Fridge and held one over the pan to tap it with the back of a knife.

It exploded.

That one got to him! "Why me, Lord?" he asked of the ceiling – which had a bit of egg detritus here and there, as did the walls, cabinets, etc. He could smell that his hair was a little singed. He didn't think it was enough to show much.

Why didn't he react in a normal fashion to these things that happened that were so far from normal it was ridiculous? Was it his determination that God would have to come up with more and more things that were weirder and weirder to even get his attention?

He sighed and picked up the other egg. It didn't explode, at least. He held it away this time.

He went to the 'Fridge and got another egg. He inspected it. It was just an egg. He tapped it, and had his omelet base. He put in the other things and put it on the stove and poured another cup of coffee. This time, he made damned sure it was a sugar cube.

When the omelet was just right he rolled his eyes and turned it.

Okay! What was this shit? It turned like he was a professional!

"Oh, no! I'm am *not* going to believe anything has changed! You got me too many times before that way!" he declared.

The omelet was good. That was part of the scheme to get him to feeling his luck (or whatever) was changing. Not gonna work!

He finished the light breakfast, dressed, and went to work. He was an expert computer programmer. At least, his luck was normal in that. He couldn't support himself if that went the way everything else did.

Lunch time. He went to the café, Nancy's, where he sometimes ate. He would rather use the restaurant four blocks away, but it looked just enough like rain that he knew he'd get there just in time for the cloudburst of the century when he started back. He was onto a lot of it.

The food was okay, but the grease seemed a bit rancid they used to cook the French fries. He covered the taste with catsup – which he should have paid more attention to when he grabbed the bottle. It was half hot sauce and half catsup, by the taste.

No go, God! I like picante!

He finished, having sense enough to forego dessert in the place. It ranged from fair to horrible. He knew from long experience which one he'd get.

He got back to his office and was going into his cubicle when he had a sudden urgent need of the toilet. It was occupied, but Fledgers came out fairly quickly. He dashed in and sat. Lots of gas, lots of noise, lots of stink.

"Good one, God. You're getting sneakier."

He went back to his cubicle, warning the three others there that he may have to make emergency runs to the toilet. Beware!

"Ate at Nancy's on Monday? Thought you knew better!" Syd chided.

"I do. I forgot it's Monday. It was just like any day since I got up."

He finished the work day. Not much of note happened, except the comp crashed when he had two hours of work on it to be lost. He was able to reformat it fast enough, since he had all the basic right there to program in again.

He got home and fixed a light dinner, SSS – the gas and such hadn't been but the one time. He dressed and looked at himself in the mirror. Other than a burned patch in his hair on the right front, he didn't look too bad.

He felt trepidation. This day had turned into one that was actually pleasant since the gas bout. He could expect the roof to fall in at any moment.

He got to Jennie's place barely on time – to find that there was no one there.

What now? She would have called if anything happened. He hoped nothing had happened to her.

He took out his cell phone to call her. It was discharged. She had probably called him and got no response.

He went back home to put the phone on the charger and to call her. She answered and said she tried to call, but his phone was off. She called at his work. Some guy named Ralph said he'd pass the message on. She had to go to Memphis. Her mother had a heart attack and was critical.

Ralph had probably written a terse note and put it on his desk and forgotten it.

He considered going somewhere.

He'd have one drink and come back home. Birthdays weren't ever that much to him.

He went into the Palm Room at the Tropical Inn Hotel. He got a Cuba Libre and went out onto the terrace. There was an attractive woman at a table, alone. He went to start a conversation. Her boyfriend came up just after he'd said he was Phil. Would she like some company?

She did react to him like she was interested. More than interested. She answered that she was with someone, thank you. She managed to slip him a phone number. He read the slip when he went back inside. Jill Ames, 555-8886.

Way to go!

He went back to finish his drink. He talked to the bartender, Jack. As he was finishing the drink

Jill walked by and gave him a look when the boyfriend was paying the tab. He smiled.

When they went on, Jack came to say, "She's expensive and will steal anything loose. We don't like her working this place. She should be down around the pool halls in Pottertown."

It figured. He went home and to bed.

On the way home a taxi went through a puddle and splashed a lot of mud on him.

Happy fucking birthday!

In the morning, which was just a *little* better than the day before, Phil was whipping up pancakes when there was a knock on the door. He sighed. If it was that nut who hinted he'd like to get him in bed he was going to knock him on his ass! He thought it was plain enough he wasn't interested.

It wasn't him. It was some guy in a cheap suit. Probably begging. He was fit enough to work, so he wouldn't get a dime from Phil Fethers.

"I'm here on an investigation," he said quickly, noting the odd look on Phil's face. "Gordon Mills. Washington and Lincoln Investigative services.

"What this is about is going to seem crazy to you. It does to me and I'm investigating it. It's about, believe it or not, chickens.

"I saw that this place has a lot of chickens wandering around and that it's not fenced with anything to keep them in or out. I need to know if any not yours have shown up the past few days.

"I know this will sound loopy. I don't know what it's about. I usually look for people or drugs or laundered money or whatever. Chickens is a first."

"I don't have any chickens, so don't pay much attention to them. There are a lot of things in the yard they like. It's the biggest lot this side of town and has two acres with nothing there. The chickens have nests around so I get all the fresh eggs I want. I don't mind having chicken gumbo or fried chicken once in awhile, either. They don't belong to anybody.

"Come on in. I'm fixing breakfast and will have to get to work right away. Maybe you can tell me what it's really about. Chickens, I won't swallow! They're just ... oh."

"Oh?"

"Would these chickens lay eggs that explode?"

"You're putting me on becuase you think I'm putting you on. I swear I'm not."

"FBI asking me about chickens doesn't make sense. FBI asking about chickens that lay exploding eggs almost does, considering what this country has become."

"I'm not FBI. I'm an independent investigator. It's not the FBI who hired me. It's another organization. I don't know why the FBI doesn't handle it."

Phil poured Gordon a cup of coffee and sat. He had to hear this one's story!

"Okay. Washington and Lincoln. How very original. It's not FBI, it's CIA. They aren't supposed to be inside the country. You're looking for chickens. I may know something. Whether or not I'll share the information depends on your answers.

"What do you know and what do you suspect. I can tell you're not sure whether or not you want anything to do with whatever it is."

"Fair enough. You're right about it being the CIA. I don't know anything about it except that a truckload of experimental chickens ran off the road and the cage door on one side came open. They got all but fourteen of the chickens. It was across Hiway Nine from here. You have those chickens. They're flock animals. Likely starting place. You said something about eggs that explode. DUH!"

"Hmm. The CIA isn't allowed to do research in this country. They are. They've produced a chicken ... heh ... that lays eggs that ex ... ex ...hee, her ... plode and they ....this is rich ...heh ... I wonder if the chickens will ex ... heh ... ha! ha! The Huh! Hee!" he broke down in laughter. Gordon stared at him.

"What the Hell?"

"I just pictured Mrs. Beaver in her apron and empty smile fixing a chi, a ... chi ... chicken for, heh! Dinner. She puts it in a pa ... pan and, hee, puts it in the hot ov ... ov ... oven and it, tuh, tuh, takes the side of the huh ... house ... out! Heeee! She's standing there with her huh ... hair singed ... and ... and black around ... around the eyes ... with a ...sur .... sur ... hee ... look .... hah, ha!"

This time Gordon broke down in hilarity, too. They both laughed until they were crying.

"Some kids find a ... guh ... nest with eggs and ... thuh ... throw one at a ... at ... a car ... and ... it ...guh ... takes the wi ... winds ...shiel ... Ha,ha!"

"She looks like ... like that ... Budweiser ad where the ... hor ... horse farts ... across the ... candle ... that I saw ... before a ... a ...superbowl once. Just that ... that look! The hair fuzzed ... fuzzed out and ... heh ... singed ... and ... the expression ... ha, ha!"

"The driver ... sitting there ... with, guh ... that same ... expres .... expression! Ha! Like Wily Coyote when a buh buh bomb ex ... exp ...ha, ha!!"

They finally were able to control their laughter and sat back. They laughed so hard and so much Phil's lungs were aching. He wiped the tears off with the dish towel. They didn't say anything for a couple of minutes. They didn't dare!

"I wonder how they worded the request for the ... the ... heh ... grant!" Gordon asked. "Gentlemen

– please give us ten million dollars so we can ... guh ... produce a chicken that ... that lays ... guh ... exploding ... hee! ... eggs! It'll save hav ... having to manu ... manufacture hand grenades!" They sat and giggled.

"I would like to know what was the object. It seems a bit odd, even for the CIA," Phil said. "I guess we'd better catch the ones laying the eggs, though. It was really a pretty forceful explosion. You can see the egg all over the room. I guess if the shell hit you edgewise it would cut."

"I have a thing that will tell me which ones. I think ... do you have a place to keep them?"

"Yeah. We can put wire across the woodshed. There's no wood in it."

"I want to see if I can find out what that bunch of clowns are doing before I give them their chickens back. I'd like to hear the explanations. They'll probably be funnier than this."

They went out back where the chickens were picking around. Gordon took a meter with an antenna sticking out of it from his pocket and turned it on. It immediately started beeping.

Phil said he had to get to work. He showed Gordon the roll of chicken wire and the shed, then dressed and went.

When he came home there were twelve chickens in the shed. Four ordinary looking roosters and eight ordinary looking hens. Gordon had taken four orange crates and had made nests in them. Maybe he'd soon have his own collection of exploding eggs.

What in hell would he do with them?

He went in the house and fixed his dinner, then thought about the program he was working on, then watched some boring TV until he went to bed early.

The morning had been mixed. He'd slipped on a shoe and had a bruised elbow where it hit the dresser on the way down. The toilet was clogged again. There was some kind of obstruction in the drain.

He thought of flushing an egg. Maybe it would explode when it hit the obstruction. He could picture the water shooting out of the toilet and pictured someone sitting on a toilet when an egg exploded in the drain. He would be sitting on one of those Disney-like spouts with the weird surprised look. He giggled. Now he was going to think about exploding eggs when anything came up.

He had just finished breakfast when Gordon came in from the back carrying two eggs. "Want some fried eggs?" he asked. They both laughed.

"I didn't find much of anything," Gordon

reported. "I have to do it with hints and suggestions. I was talking with the person who gave me the assignment. I said I had some hints that one person had a lot more chickens this week than she had three weeks ago. I asked if I should just poison them or something. He called a number and some Dr. Bossman came to ask about what I found. I just said it was a remark, but that was how I would find anything. Anybody who suddenly had a dozen more laying hens was going to try to see no one knew.

"He said I was not to harm the chickens. They needed them to finish the research, so I suggested I would find them and just break any eggs they'd laid to be sure whoever had them didn't raise the chicks and breed their own whatever.

"I was told, very nervously, that I was to handle any eggs with extreme care. That's what they really need from the hens. He gave me a number to call immediately if I found any. He would come to gather the eggs, himself. In person. To see there was no lost research, don't you know, Old Sock! It didn't seem to occur to him that anyone who had the eggs would sell them or cook them. People don't just leave them there in the nests."

"They live in some kind of fantasy world. Maybe we can arrange to find one of the hens and where she had laid a couple eggs. You could call him. I would very naturally want to know why some scientist guy wanted my chickens and eggs. It might be fun to hear the story."

"Or it might occur to them you know too much already, so they should eliminate that kind of problem before it cropped up. Be careful. I know those people and the way they, excuse the expression, think."

"I can thwart them in that. I'm not the kind of person they're used to dealing with."

They made a plan. Gordon and Phil were going to be buddies and a team. Phil didn't fall for that one, either ... still, Gordon had the hens and eggs, so he would tend to handle the problem if he was that type.

"Why, wouldn't it be a streak of fantastic luck for them to have found a computer genius who could save them years in their resrach?" he asked, innocently.

Gordon grinned and giggled. "What would be your guarantee that you wouldn't accidentally give them some kind of idea that might work?"

"Not in the equation. If you knew me, you'd see that!

"Let's work out how we do it."

Phil had always had a very large supply of luck. He was known to admit it and to say it was a pity it was all bad. He was going to go way out on a limb and trust that it would continue as it always had been.

He called Jennie to ask how she was doing. She said she was going to be stuck in Memphis for at least a month. She would appreciate it if he would take care of her place. Feed the goldfish and that kind of thing. The yard wasn't big, so it wouldn't be hard to maintain. He could stay there if he liked. She trusted him. He was her closest friend in all the world.

He agreed. She said the key to the back door was under the pot of begonias by the steps. The other keys, the spare set, were in the cutlery drawer in the kitchen, first on the left of the stove.

Damn it! This wasn't his bad luck streak!

He knew what to do! He called Gordon and said to meet him tonight. They were going to move a chicken and a couple of eggs to a new home. He had time coming. They would arrange for Gordon to call Dr. Bossman tomorrow to come try to convince him he should be allowed to take the chickens. Gordon said he found out about these, but couldn't just steal them or anything because too many people would ask too many questions. It was his job to find the chickens. He said to call him when he did. It was now up to him.

Phil moved one hen and one rooster to Jennie's back yard. He and Gorden spent a little time making a cage with a wooden box for a roost. The smaller box with the nest was inside. He bought a sack of chicken feed. Phil managed to hit his thumb with a hammer and to cut his other hand with a saw and to tear his pants on a nail and spill water down the front of his pants that looked like he'd pissed in them. Everything was perfectly normal.

They decided to call Bossman at seven thirty. Gordon would say; "... was waiting when he got home from work. He says he has a chicken. Two. He caught them beside a public road and isn't about to give them to anybody. He can have a fresh egg every morning from his own back yard! He doesn't need money. He's damned suspicious why anybody would offer a hundred bucks apiece for chickens he caught by the side of the road. There were a dozen there, at least. He told me to fuck off."

"Dr. Bossman, I agreed to find the chickens. The

rest is up to you. I'm going out where he caught them to see if I can find them."

"No way! Half the town knows about them. He'll probably tell them about me offering a hundred bucks apiece. Half the town will be out there tomorrow to try to catch a hundred dollar chicken!"

"If I did that, you'd really have some questions you dare not answer. I'm not about to put my neck on that block!"

"I'll tell him you'll be here. I don't think he works tomorrow, or that he'll work here. He's a research computer expert or something. The way he talked, he knows exactly who I am. I talked to him at five at his office, he's said some things that no one knows."

"He's a *computer* expert. He can find anything it would take us a month to find in ten minutes."

"I'll run over and tell him."

"I can think of a lot of ways that would solve more than one problem. Who knows. He might be able to save you ten years of research because you asked the right question the right way or something."

"I'll be out there at dawn. I may be able to find the rest of them."

He hung up and grinned. "He'll be here about nine in the morning. I think he'll want to hire you, which means he would get the chickens and maybe the one who could help him make the breakthrough of the century in genetic splicing. We know how they're doing it. We have to learn why."

"I worry. Things are going right. They never do."

"What the Hell? Like you finding chickens by the road. Maybe you could find facts by the computer. Tell him you're at the point in your work where you could make thousands a week from the contracts. He'll offer thousands a week to work for him, plus you would be free to pursue your own path part time, is the way he put it."

"Where will he get thousands a week to pay me?"

"Same place he gets his. The taxpaying schmucks."

Phil gave him the old one finger salute.

"Yes? That Gordon character said you would come today to explain why you want my damned chickens."

Dr. Bossman was a short, plump man with salt and pepper hair who wore steel frame glasses. His clothes didn't quite fit him. He had a soldier bring him in a military Jeep.

"Yes, yes," he replied testily. "They're research

subjects that escaped from a truck. I hope you have not eaten any of the eggs from those chickens. It could be, er, dangerous. Chemical contamination, you see. It's why we have to get them all back.

"You said there were more than a dozen? You told Gordon exactly where they were?"

"Yeah. It was several days ago. They're probably all over the county now, the ones that haven't ended up as somebody's chicken soup."

"Oh, I hope not!" he cried. "Well, eating the chickens themselves probably wouldn't hurt anyone. It's the eggs that are of concern."

"Why?"

"If you break them open they could, uh, release a very toxic gas. Or something. Nobody must open one of those eggs!"

"Well, I didn't check the nest the last couple of days.. Chickens will stop laying if they have a fright or something. We can see if this one's laid any."

He led Bossman out to the little cage. They went in and to the nest. Where there were two eggs they put in yesterday, there were now three.

"They are laying eggs! Oh, dear! Oh, dear!"

Phil reached into the nest and got the three eggs. They headed back to the house. Phil put the eggs in a plastic container and set them on the porch rail. Bossman said he would take the eggs to the Jeep and would return to tell Phil how important their research was. Phil handed the container to Bossman. He managed to slip just then and one egg rolled out of the container (with his help) and across the concrete post by the steps. He grabbed for it. Bossman held the container like it would try to escape by itself.

The egg rolled off the post and fell the two or three feet below the porch level to land in a clump of fern. The fern was in the rocks. The path went down from there for another two steps before the level ground. The egg rolled out and dropped on a rock by the path.

There was an explosion a little more forceful than when he tapped the egg. Bossman squealed like a stuck pig. Phil faked a surprised-shocked look.

Phil turned to Bossman. "I think the explanation for that isn't going to be easy to swallow. Shall we go inside and have a little talk?"

Bossman called the soldier and gave him the two remaining eggs. The soldier asked about the explosion he just heard. Bossman said he demonstrated a thing for use in running crows away from crops. Those eggs were part of the research. Handle them with extreme care. Phil and he went inside, where Phil poured them each a cup of coffee.

"Well?"

"I am a geneticist. We spliced genes into the chickens that produce two very reactive chemicals. They are sensitive to shock and will react from a shock that would break the hell. The research from that point is to make the shells contain a compound much like an acrylic. It would then be...."

"... making the explosion throw six very sharp, hard blades at high velocity. The blades could easily kill the person cracking the egg," Phil explained to Gordon.

"Cripes! What would they do with anything like that?"

"Use them for assassinations of terrorist leaders, anywhere. He gets up, does the SSS bit, then goes into the kitchen to have his breakfast. A good percent of the time that includes eggs. Boom. One less problem for our government, no connection. Oh, boo-hoo."

"Would it work?"

"Yes, except for the little detail that kind of idiot always misses."

"Such as?"

"How many powerful world leaders go in the kitchen in the morning to cook their own breakfast? Maybe they could kill off the leaders' chefs."

They were going to get the giggles again. Gordon changed the subject. "So? What's the offer to you?"

"Well, he has his limits. I projected I would make five thousand a week from what I'm working on. He said that was within the budget. I could continue with what I was working on in my spare time, which would be most of it. They will give me room, board, and all that, plus the five grand is tax exempt.

"I said I'd consider it."

"Will you?"

"Sure! Two months at that and I'll have enough to do several things I want to do."

"Ah-ah! Careful! Once in, you can never get out. That's why I'm an independent contractor."

"Which is just what I'd be."

"You'll still know too much. Be careful."

Phil nodded seriously.

Now to see where this fiasco would lead. The one thing certain about it was that it would supply enough laughs for enough years to be worth it. Phil did always retain his sense of humor and the ridiculous. He laughed a lot.

After Bossman left he had gone back to his place. He had seven eggs in the nest boxes there.

He wondered if they had a long shelf life. That

gave him the giggles again. He wandered around, fixed a few things around the house he had been putting off, then went back to Jennie's to feed the chickens. He pulled a few weeds in her spice garden.

He was stuck wondering what to do with his time. He could maybe set up a website for the independant farmers.

Chicken farmers? It would have a forum and blogs. That could get Bossman's bowels in an uproar! He could put a test run question something like: *I would like some advice from those who raise chickens commercially.*

I raise corn for the cattle feed industry and admit I don't know much about chickens. Several chickens wandered into my barn, I guess because of all that corn, and stayed. It was okay. I like eggs as much as the next guy, and chicken soup is a good change now and then.

What I want to know is if their shit or something can explode. They stay in the loft at night and have nests in the hay up there. Two times something has blown up. It's costing me a lot to have to fix all that stuff. How do you keep that from happening? Is it something in their diet? I heard about feeding them gunpowder, but always thought that was just a tale.

Would that cause a panic or what?

He got the giggles. He pictured some farmer going out to the barn in the morning and finding a big hole where a whole nest full of eggs exploded and took the roof off. The tractor looked like a bazooka hit it!

Would Bossman read something like that and believe it? What would he do?

Let's see. The eggs explode with a force of a quarter stick of fifty percent dynamite. If there were three eggs and one fell out of the loft it would explode. That wouldn't be enough ... oh, dear me! The concussion would cause the other eggs in the building to detonate! Oh, dear me! I never figured on something like this! They weren't supposed to have their nests in a loft! Let me see. If we raise a thousand hens and they all lay an egg and we store them in a warehouse, what happens if someone drops one right there in the building? Oh, dear me! It would be like when the arsenal in Iraq went up! It would take out a city block, at least!

Oh, well. We'll just be sure we raise them where there aen't any close neighbors. Problem solved!

Phil shook his head. That would be about the reaction he could expect. About two days later he would stop all of a sudden. "Oh, dear me! That means we didn't find all of those chickens when the truck turned over! They're breeding! This could be worse than killer bees!"

The CIA would have to come up with a cover story. There would have to be a goat.

Well, they probably had one. They would think of that-

News Date

Pres. Bossman of the Washington and Lincoln Research center in Podunk, Mississippi, has been arrested and charged with being a mad scientist. The recent scare because of a few silly pitiful incidents with exploding eggs has been traced to Dr. Bossman, who had some wild and crazy scheme from his fevered insanity to take over the army by producing chickens that lay eggs that will explode. No one can understand the reasoning behind the insane idea.

"While Dr. Bossman has done some independent contract work with government agencies, he does not and did not represent any agency that operates within the borders of the United States of America and I didn't know anything about it, so you sure as heck can't blame me for anything I did't ever even dream was happening!" President Smith answered forcefully when asked if he was aware of the incidents. "I had not heard anything about this before your questions here. I have asked congress to investigate the matter. I imagine what work he

did was for the administration before mine. You are aware of the depths to which that party will sink. They will undoubtably attempt to charge this administration with something or other, but I tell you right now it will be false and that such specious charges will come to nothing."

We will report immediately on any further developments in the case.

In other words, you could expect typical political double-talk. It won't occur to any of the reporters to ask how he has congress investigating something he didn't know about until their questions right there.

He went back to his place. He was a bit nervous about his long spate of normal to good luck. The higher he got, the longer and harder the fall.

He locked Jennie's place carefully, then went out the front gate. He heard someone call his name and looked up as he was closing it and managed to slam it on his hand. He looked around, but didn't see anyone who had called to him.

A truck was dumping a load of topsoil on a lawn down the block. He probably heard someone calling about where to dump the fill or something.

He turned toward his place and stepped on something that almost dumped him on his ass. Dog shit! He swore rather colorfully and looked up from the crap to see the four from the church standing there with shocked looks on their faces.

Nothing to lose now. "People who let their damned dogs shit on the fucking sidewalk should be horsewhipped," he said pleasantly. He walked on. He heard the one who had come back to his house say, "It's a test from God. It has to be!"

A kid on a bicycle flew around the corner where a hedge cut off the view and knocked him down. He couldn't very well knock a seven or eight year old girl on her ass. He said she shouldn't be riding her bike on the sidewalk.

She said, "Fuck you! " Got on her bike, and rode away.

Hell! A big black streak down his pans!

It started raining. It wasn't an ordinary rain, it was the storm of the year. It had to be!

He dashed across the street and slipped on the wet sidewalk on the corner, falling into two trash cans there. One had some rotten meat or something in it that smelled like ... rotten meat.

He got up and said, "Welcome back, God! I missed you!"

Why did he get a feeling of comradery? He was as nuts as a loon!

He managed to survive the rest of the way home. He'd left two windows open. The bedroom was soaked.

Yep! Things were back to normal! He wouldn't turn a hair if lightning struck all those exploding eggs out back and made a mess of the neighborhood.

He pictured a snow of feathers. The chickens were right there. It would solve the chicken roundup.

He plugged in the coffee pot. It made a "pffffttt" sound and burned out.

He sighed and put the coffee in a pan of water and put it on the stove.

No gas. As much as expected. It didn't bother him. He took out a hotplate and put the pan on it. He had two more he got on sale when Harpner's went out of business.

"God, you just have to come up with something new. This is getting boring."

He cooked a steak from the Fridge on the hotplate and ate it with a bag of soggy potato chips and some wilted lettuce salad. He then puttered around the computer for awhile, then showered and went to bed. It had been quite a day!

There must have been a bitch in heat close. A pack of dogs spent three hours barking and fighting all over the property until he went out with his slingshot and popped a couple of them. They went down the property to where they could keep him awake without being in range of his slingshot. He contemplated getting the .22 out and picking about ten of them off.

He'd end up in jail for discharging a firearm in an occupied area. He knew better.

He went back to bed. Those damned dogs would bark all night. He was thinking of poisoning every dog in the neighborhood, which he would never do, as tempting as it seemed at the moment. He smirked to himself and put on a bathrobe, then went out to the woodshed. There were four eggs in the nests.

He threw one toward the dogs. He had a good arm. It hit right in the middle of the pack.

Oh, shit! He ran into the house and turned on a light in the bedroom, then went out front to look down the road toward the corpses of four or five dogs scattered along the road. The neighbor from that end across the road was just coming to his gate.

The best defense ... "What did you do, Tom?" he called. "Whatever that was, you should get the citizenship medal. Those damned dogs were driving me crazy! If the cops come or anything, I'll say a car went by, there was a 'boom' and it kept right on going."

"I didn't do anything! I was thinking of ... maybe it happened just like that. Whatever, it got rid of some of them! I wish it could have been twenty more of them!"

"Yeah. Whoever, I'll pay for another grenade if they'll use it! I wish I had the guts!"

They chatted a few minutes. No cops came. They decided the county truck would pick the dogs up in the morning.

This time, Phil managed to get to sleep. He would tell Gordon he found a good use for the eggs in the morning.

Phil was fixing his eggs (not those) for breakfast when Bossman and Gordon came rushing in. Bossman said there was the sound of an explosion last night. It was on this property – and why wasn't he at the house where they'd talked?

"A bitch in heat had dogs barking all night. Tom or somebody threw a grenade at them." Gordon was behind Bossman and grinned at Phil, who wasn't having complete success at hiding his laughter. Bossman didn't seem to notice.

"The truck with the chickens turned over just a few hundred feet from here, on Hiway nine," Bossman said. "We feared something ... but it's a relief to know it wasn't that."

"It could have been," Phil pointed out. "The dogs running around. A nest in the grass. Boom!"

"Gheeee!"

"I wasn't at the other place last night because my girlfriend who lives there is in Memphis. I live here. I take care of her place when she's away sometimes."

"But why did you take the chickens there? There are a lot of them outside here right now!"

"Because these aren't mine. I can keep mine in a cage there and the eggs are mine. Not that I want those particular eggs."

"Oh. I see. Well, I suppose Gordon checked all of these, so they aren't very ... but then, where did the egg that the dogs broke come from?"

"That was only a possibility. The chickens come and go. Maybe one came and went."

"I'll check the ones outside," Gordon said. He went out. Phil offered coffee to Bossman, who sat at the table and looked harried. He said he wished he'd never heard of those damned particular genes.

"Dr. Bossman, how would you store the eggs? Would they retain their potency?"

"Oh, refrigerate them and they aren't sensitive. The chemicals will break down naturally in about three weeks without refrigeration. We worked out everything that can happen."

"Except for a truck that runs off the road."

"Yes. That was unforeseen. I hope it is the only thing. I have some hesitation before inserting the acrylic-producing gene."

They chatted a bit. Gordon came in with a hen and a rooster. He said they had wandered in sometime. Maybe that's where the dog egg came from. There were fourteen lost. They had two here and two at the other place, which meant they only had to find ten more. That was to tell Phil this probably accounted for all of them. There were ten in the woodshed. There was a question about one hen unaccounted for, but that was just a difference on the manifest and more than likely didn't mean anything.

"I guess we'd better get on back. I'll come here this afternoon to see if any more wander in. I'll spend this morning checking out things I've heard," Gordon suggested, rolling his eyes toward Bossman.

Yeah. It would be a good idea to get him out of there before he thought of looking over the place.

Phil walked them to the door. He saw the other three eggs from last night on the table there. Gordon spotted them and pointed to water in the hall, drawing Bossman's attention. He said there was water there. Phil said it was an open window with yesterday's rain. He was going to mop it up this morning.

They got Bossman out without him spotting the eggs.

They drove off. Phil went with them to the Jeep. There was still some mud around, so he got some on him when the wheels spun in a puddle.

"Good to know I can depend on you, God! Good morning!" He went back inside. He took the mattress from the big bed outside into the sunlight. It was soaked through. It would take a couple of days to dry out. Lucky he had the guest room to stay in until things were back to as close to normal as they would get.

He remembered those eggs. He put them in the Fridge. Bossman said they were safe if they were cold.

He slammed the door to the Fridge. The eggs weren't cold yet. There was a loud "Mmmppfth!" sound and the door flew open. The sides of the Fridge were puffed out slightly. The insulation absorbed most of the shock.

"Shit!" he said, dejectedly.

He cleaned up the mess. The door fit alright. It sealed. The Frdige looked a bit weird, sort of rounded. It seemed to keep right on working. Only one of the eggs exploded, it seemed. Not all of those hens were laying the spliced eggs. It did blow all the stuff in the Fridge into a gooey mess of a ball.

"You're going to have to think up things that don't make such a mess. I could get irritated."

He finally had the place in good shape and clean. Gordon came and said he had no choice about those two chickens. The driver saw him catch them. No loss.

"Yeah. I did find a good use for them. I can tell you the eggs aren't so easy to set off if they're cold, but I guess you knew that. Don't put them in the refrigerator and slam the door. Wait until they're cold for that. I can also tell you not all of them will explode."

Gordon looked at the Fridge. He shook his head, then couldn't hide a giggle. Phil giggled in turn, then they laughed and made up scenarios where the eggs exploded. Gordon decided he'd "find" one or two chickens a day.

Tom called the county about the dead dogs. They picked them up. The man on the truck asked if he could expect more. Tom told him he hoped so, but they didn't know who bombed them. They would buy him another grenade or two.

"They won't be back tonight. They form packs when there's a bitch in heat. That would be the black and white one. She got the hardest hit."

"That works as well, " Phil said. "Just so we can get some sleep. They ought to make people keep their dogs home."

"That's the law, but nobody pays it any mind. It works alright. They won't make too much of a stink if you reduce the canine population. Claim their dog, pay a fifty buck fine."

Phil went to Jennie's to feed his chickens and be sure everything was alright in the house. He got a new tank of gas for the stove at home and bought a few things he needed. He decided he was going to make five grand a week, so he bought a good mattress. The delivery truck was there so he rode home with the new mattress. It was a good one, and expensive. OrthoPerfect model A100. Eight hundred thirty nine bucks!

He thoroughly expected that he wasn't going to get the job, now that he spent the money.

What the Hell? He had enough saved up that it wouldn't hurt.

He worked around the yard for a couple of hours, then went in to fix lunch. He flipped on the TV to see "... this OrthoPerfect model A100 for only three hundred fifty dollars, today only! Less than half the original price! Limited number in stock!"

Okay! The job would probably be there. He lost about what could be expected if things were truly back to what was normal for him. He was learning how to use what was happening to him.

Don't get smug.

He hooked up the gas tank, or started to. This tank was from another distributor and didn't fit his regulator.

He took the other regulator and hose from the drawer, hooked it up, and had the stove again. Another place where he was prepared for things that were bound to happen to him.

"You're slipping! Old lady driving you up the

walls, God?"

Maybe he had one like those old Greek gods. A haridan of a wife. He giggled at the thought. He could picture Michaelangelo's God saying, "It ain't funny!" with a miserable look on his face.

He reached into the cabinet for the flour. He moved his hand around until he hit the mouse trap. Pain time! It was a good thing it wasn't a rat trap! That would have broken fingers instead of just hurting.

A lot of these thing were from his own mind. He knew the trap was there. He knew to close the windows before he left.

A lot weren't. He had to pay more attention to his own shortcomings to get much relief. He had to be wary about those things he didn't do to himself.

He went to the woodshed to collect the seven eggs there. He was careful when he put them in the Fridge. No slamming doors.

He had the whole afternoon. He would go fishing.

He got to the lake on the bus. He walked to where he liked to fish where he sat on the log there to rig his reel. The log had rotted enough on the end that it dropped off the rock and dumped him in the mud. He swore. This was going to be a normal – for him – trip.

He saw some swirls a little to the left and went through the willows to be able to cast into the action on the water. The first cast tangled in the branches above him. He got it worked loose and made a perfect cast into the action. Strke!

He pulled in a carp. No good! He turned it loose.

He cast a few more time. He got another strike, but the line broke and he lost his favorite lure.

He headed back to his spot. He slipped on a rock by the water and ended up in the lake. He climbed out to get tangled in the willow branches. He worked his way to the log. His cap was missing.

He saw it floating out into the lake. Shit!

He cast a few times, then changed lures again.

First cast he caught a nice bass he put on a stringer. He cast a few more times and got a strong hit. He fought the fish in.

A catfish? They almost never hit top water lures!

Oh, well. He threw it back and sat on the log (he had put another rock under the hard part) to have a cold beer, only it wasn't cold. The ice had melted and run out. When he opened it the foam kept spewing out all over his arm and hand. He ate some soggy cheese crackers with it.

He moved around a bit, but didn't see any likely spots, so went back to the log. His stringer was gone.

There were several kids playing around the area.

He should have known better than to leave if far.

He fished some more and caught another bass. He made a stringer with a piece of polypropylene he carried. He moved around a bit more, not going where he couldn't see the stringer. He made a few more casts, but nothing was biting. He got a backlash that made knots of the nylon. He swore and worked on it for a minute, then swore again. He decided to go back home.

The first bus got one look at him as it stopped. The door closed in his face and it drove off. He gave it the one finger salute.

A half hour later the bus stopped. He was prepared with a big black garbage bag, so put it on the seat to sit on. The driver thanked him for being considerate of other people. About two percent of his riders were.

When he got home a little after five he was drenched and muddy and his favorite fishing shirt was beyond salvation. He'd lost his lucky fishing cap. He reel was jambed up with nylon in hundreds of knots. His favorite lure was gone.

And with a nice bass for supper. There was always that one tiny redeeming factor.

He would cut the nylon from the reel and put on new. He had several old shirts for fishing, as well as pants. His only loss that he cared about was his fishing cap, but he caught his supper after it was lost. He caught supper on another lure.

All in all, another ho-hum day.

He piddled around, got another egg from the woodshed, worked on the farm website, watched fifteen minutes of stupidly extreme karate and bombs and bullets, and went to bed. The mattress smelled new, but was as comfortable as advertised.

Why hadn't Gordon come back?

He reached for the phone to call. There was no answer.

He laid back down. Three minutes later the phone rang.

It was Jennie. She just got the strangest call. Flo Jenkins, next door to her place there, said there was some kind of explosion at her place and something about dead chickens. What was that about?

"I don't know. Maybe ... an explosion? Chickens?

"I put two chickens in a little cage I made there until Gordon, a friend, could pick them up to take to, uh, his place out of town. I was fishing at the lake until five or so. I hadn't heard anything about any explosion. I was there this morning to check things out and to feed the chickens.

"That big white lily thing by the steps is blooming. I guess you'll miss it. It only blooms for a week or so. I'll take a picture and e-mail it to you." Change the subject and see what the Hell was going on!

She chattered about how she knew he would take better care of her place than she did. Blah, blah, boring blah. After ten minutes or ten hours or eternity he was able to get her off the phone.

Should he go to her place?

Tomorrow.

He went back to bed.

He got up to no aches and pains in the morning. That was a new one! Maybe getting rid of that old mattress was his good decision for this month!

He managed to not hurt himself seriously through breakfast, then called Gordon again. No answer.

Go to Jennie's. Find out if there's a connection.

His phone rang. It was Gordon. He said the police had his phone. He could only use it when one of them was there. He didn't have much time. Things would work out okay. His boss would get him out. He'd explain later. Charging him with animal cruelty was just plain ridiculous! He didn't know there were any chickens there! He just set off a crow bomb at dusk because the damned things were roosting in that big pecan tree! How the hell would he know Jennifer had chickens! She was in Memphis! Got to go!

That explained a lot.

He got the giggles. What had probably happened was that hen laid an egg. The nest crate was about two feet off the ground. Something had dropped the egg out of the nest. Boom!

He pictured the hen, Disney style, clucking and

laying an egg, the egg falling, and the surprised look and feathers falling all around. He pictured God again saying, "It ain't funny!" He got the giggles.

Not too much happened on the way to Jennie's. He saw the mess that had been the cage. Flo came over to ask what had happened. He said he wasn't sure. He thought a can of starting fluid blew up. It was mostly ether, you know. If the press valve leaked a little it took almost nothing to ignite ether.

She went back to her place. Phil's phone rang. Gordon was out. Bossman had pulled some strings somehow. They had to explain that explosion better than a crow bomb. They was all noise.

"I told Flo, next door, it was probably starting fluid that leaked. Ether. Boom! Get a can and take it out somewhere and make it blow, then come here and 'find' it."

"Good thinking! Done! How did you explain it being there?"

"Didn't. Maybe for the lawn mower. It's hard to start.

"How do you suppose it happened? Why were you here?"

"I wasn't far away. Bossman had a transmitter hidden there. A bug. He heard it and called me. I went over just in time for the cops to come and catch me trying to get rid of the feathers and such. I figured there might be an egg. There are too many chicken snakes around there. They eat the eggs. Probably, one got in the nest and dropped the egg out. I'll check for a dead snake."

Phil said he'd wait. He went around the place. He found a dead chicken snake about two feet long tangled in twisted chicken wire. It was easy to figure. It wasn't big enough to swallow the egg. It had tried and had knocked the egg out of the nest.

Gordon came about an hour later. He had a twisted starting fluid can that was ripped open along the seam. He tossed it among the mess and said the police would come over with Bossman in a little while. Bossman would "find" the can and explain about the lawn mower. Phil would say he bought a can and had used it once. It was back there somewhere. Maybe something turned it over and the press valve was hit, making a slow leak. Something caused a spark or whatever. So it didn't make sense. It would go down as the cause of the explosion, let's go have a beer.

"Why is your head bleeding?" Gordon asked.

"It is?" he put his hand up to his head. Gordon said the other side. There was blood.

"I suppose it was from the chicken wire when I

found the snake."

"Put some antibiotic on it."

They waited. Bossman came with a fat policeman. They went through the cage. Bossman "found" the ether can. The cop found the snake. Gordon said the can was probably on the shelf (that they couldn't say wasn't there amid the wreckage), the snake went along the shelf and knocked the can off. The can landed upside down, which broke the press valve off. It was ether. Something set it off. The cop was more than ready to make that suggestion in his report. Shake hands, say what a great job they'd done on this investigation, and go.

Gordon and Bossman were undecided as to what to do next. Bossman said they had to find the rest of those chickens. Phil said that was their problem. He would do what he could.

"Oh. Yes. Well, now that you work for us, you can aid Gordon in the search. I put you on the book as starting today."

They agreed. Bossman called his driver and left. Gordon and Phil cleaned up the mess and had the yard back to much as it had been before this fiasco.

They decided they would find the rest of the chickens today. There was no way this particular type of research could ever become practical. It would give Phil a very good start at his new job.

<u>*What Next, Lord?*</u>

Phil Fethers stretched and looked in the mirror. It was a little crooked, so he reached to straighten it. It fell off the hook and crashed to the floor. It was stainless steel, so didn't break.

"Good morning! I was onto that one years ago. Old lady giving you Hell again?"

He nicked himself shaving. He put antibiotic cream on it. No chances.

The coffee pot got knocked off the stove, but he had a full cup. He gave it the bird and turned it upright. There was still more than a cup in it. He mopped the coffee up and put the eggs on the stove. The omelet looked perfect until he turned it. It then looked like scrambled eggs with vegetables. The toaster stuck and he had two sheets of charcoal when he popped it up. He dropped them in the garbage and put in two more slices. There was a humming noise, then the lights went out.

He unplugged the toaster and went to flip on the breaker.

Today made three months at the job. He was told the job would probably end in less than six months, but that would give him time to finish his project.

He guessed so. He would start it at any minute!

Bossman was being transferred to the Arizona facility. It was too dangerous to be handled anywhere other than the desert with no one within fifty miles.

He smirked to himself. Today the computer would make it necessary for Bossman to start another project. He had checked interdepartmental to find more than twenty million dollars had been wasted on Operation Igeldy Pigeldy Project.

He sat to write the "Findings" of his special program to detect odds of a project working to specs.

The experimental insertion of genetic material into chickens is successful and has added much to scientific bases. The project is a success in producing more than was spent, though that production is in the scientific end, not the military.

The apparent success in inserts to produce an acrylic-like substance is as valuable, but for other uses.

The factors behind the original purpose of the experiments were lacking in finalization. The process was decreed practical for the production end, but the practical use end was faulty. The fact the product was there for use was negated by the fact that it was a use that was not practical. Suggest termination of project.

Factor not investigated properly: Terrorist leaders do not prepare their own food.

Phil sat back and read it over, then put it on a memory stick for his computer to find and report.

He went out front to find a group of church people coming down the road. He would be the second stop.

He got an evil grin on his face and went back inside.

There was soon a knock on his door. He went to throw the door open. Two of the women gasped and backed down the sidewalk toward the road. One gave him an appraising look, then slowly did the same. The one man with them looked like he would faint. He turned and walked away without a word.

Phil grinned and quietly closed the door. This was another bunch who wouldn't be back.

"I can play a few little tricks like this against your competition, huh?"

He got the comrady feeling for the second time. Weird.

He would look for another project. He had enough to live on for awhile. Maybe he'd make a big coop on the property and raise chickens for eggs.

Nah! He giggled at the idea.

He still needed a new project. He could probably get in with the government. He could get in touch with Gordon, who would know a few of the silly things they were up to.

He realized he was standing nude in the doorway when a car went by and swerved nearly off the road.

He went inside. He could smell ... something?

Oh. The lye. He had put half the can into the toilet. He was determined he would get it unclogged to the point it would stay unclogged. That burnt smell may mean it had burned out whatever was in the way.

He went in to see the water in the bowl bubbling almost like it was boiling. The lye was damned sure eating something away!

There was a loud gurgle, then the water went down the drain, leaving a dirty brown glop in the bottom.

He flushed it. The new water would ... blow out and all over the bathroom! It was mostly steam and vapors that left a brownish coating on everything.

Good one, Lord! I have to admit I didn't expect that one!

Did he hear a giggle?

What? You forgot I tiled this whole bathroom for just such an eventuality?

He went to the closet, took out the garden hose, hooked it to the spigot outside the back door and washed the bathroom down. It was about time to clean it, anyway.

He coiled the hose and put it back, then looked into the toilet. It should have stopped boiling by now, but it was even hotter.

Lye is a base. He got the large bottle of vinegar from the kitchen and poured some of it into the boiling water.

Oh, shit! You can't add an acid to a hot base! It'll ... it did. It got so hot it cracked the toilet.

There was another gurgle. The water went down the drain.

He would just buy another toilet. He knew how to do that kind of plumbing.

He rinsed the bathroom down again, got his tools, and took the old toilet out. He used the time to clean the area. While it was open like that he would run a snake down the line. He would be damned sure there wasn't anything obstructing it now!

See, Lord? I can turn almost any of it to a good result.

He opened the vent and left the door open with

the big fan blowing in to dry it, then headed for the dealer for a new toilet. The lavatory was dirty and old. He had the money. He bought everything new.

Phil looked at the gleaming new bathroom. He decided it was really all for the best.

Back to what he was doing when this started. He needed a new project to use his time.

He called Gordon, who said he had gotten some questions about what they had done and what he knew. He told them Phil was as good a security risk as they would ever find. He knew when to keep his mouth shut.

"Their computers told them that you were the best man to look into feasibility studies. Didn't your own program tell them that, had they gotten in touch with you beforehand, those millions spent on something with no military application would have been saved?

"If it ain't got military application they ain't interested."

"Well, I hope they ... could someone accidentally suggest having me design programs to look for things that were missed in the programs they're running now?"

"What?"

"Maybe a program that would actually give them what they're after could be found to be faulty?"

He grinned. "I've heard rumors about some crazy nuclear thing out of a horror show they're sniffing around. A couple of really top scientists are very worried about it because it could work.

"From what I heard, it could kill all animal life and not damage the buildings or plants or whatever. The one I overheard was saying it had a range of almost a mile. The problem would be finding a way to keep it in a sharp focus. They were saying something about director magnets and damper coils."

Phil shrugged. They went to his computers. He checked the secret coded databases he'd learned about with the egg job, as he called it. There really was something like that proposed.

He checked finances/military/research. If it was Project Flashlight, there was already four million spent on primary research.

He introduced a secondary file. It was something they would find. Something that had been there all along, but was ignored. He put in a key that would come up within a day.

The net went down. He was sure it had been sent.

Lord, if you're doing that, this is too serious for games, okay?

The net came back online. That really did shock him.

Nah!

He worked a bit, then went in to fix dinner. Gordon had left an hour ago.

There was some stuff in the Fridge. He opened the door. The smell of rotted meat almost knocked him down.

He hadn't been home yesterday. He didn't get anything from it last night or this morning.

He sighed. He needed a new one, anyhow. It could have waited until after lunch.

He had some bread. Moldy.

A can of tuna and some egg noodles later he headed for the appliance store. He bought a new Fridge with a larger freezer.

When he got home there was a man standing by the door. A man in a cheap dark blue suit with black patent leather shoes.

"Mr. Fethers?"

"Yeah. Come on in. Tell me what it's about. Try to string me and you get nowhere."

He looked at Phil, then shrugged. "I'm Nort Green. What gave me away?"

"You're wearing a goddamned uniform! What the hell do you mean?"

"But ... oh. You worked with us. You know ... it isn't important. I wasn't going to try to snow you. I just have to ask you to do a little job for the department. They want to know something about the feasibility of research. We feel you could possibly save us a lot of time and funding if the projects won't produce more than they cost."

"You should have had that program going for years. You would have a lot of stuff you don't have and would probably have a few billion to play around with.

"The Flashlight Project kind of thing?"

"I don't know what. I ... never heard of that one. That could mean it's what it's about. You know how we operate. I'll check. It should shake somebody up if you know about it."

He took out a large cell phone and made a call. He went down the sidewalk a distance. He gave Phil a strange look, then came to hand him the phone.

"Mr. Fethers, just where did you hear about the *non-existent* Flashlight Project?"

"On the net. There was some stuff on a forum or something."

There was a long silence. Phil shrugged and was handing the phone back to Nort when the voice continued.

"The net? It was on the net?"

"Yeah. Somewhere. I just mentioned that one. There was talk about Project Silk Purse and HAARP and all that."

"Silk Purse? I don't ... but those are top secret!

So is Flashlight!"

"That kind of thing is on the web as soon as someone thinks of it. (Phil had an idea. This would be fun!) England with their 'Derby Hat' Project and their New Flower Project and such. France with the Fleu de Lis and Germany with Ach Tung! and Russia with Yastrovia are out months before the departments they go to have a hint. Governments can't hide that kind of thing when they don't understand how the net works."

"We've got to be able to shut the net down! That's all there is to it!"

"And you'd then be the only ones who didn't have a way to check on what anyone else is doing. Even a feasibility program half as sophisticated as mine would tell you that."

"How do we fight it?"

"By having someone who does understand it show you how to keep the information from being on the web in a usable form. Information carries its own tags, you know. You have to be able to avoid the tags and you can keep it secret for a little while."

"You can do that?"

"I haven't thought about it. I suppose so. It would be the best defense you could think of, really. I never thought about it much."

"When can you come to work? It will have to be

where we can keep it secret!"

"Which would be a tag an idiot would find in ten seconds. It doesn't get through to you that's exactly the thing that identifies a project?"

There was a whimper.

"I work here at home. Nobody suspects a thing. I'm just cruising the forums and blogs, as always."

"But they wouldn't ever know that you weren't at home!" he cried triumphantly.

"Ever heard of an IPO?"

"Er?"

"Every time you go online there is a record. An IPO (He wasn't sure that was the right one, but this idiot certainly wouldn't!) is registered. It's international information. If some new one goes onto the forums it can be traced. An old one like mine is ignored."

"We don't have computers that get around that?"

"No. No registration, no use of the net. It's automatic and built into the machines. The best way to hide some kinds of things is the purloined letter."

"Is that some kind of program we can use?"

"You don't know what ... no. It's a psychological system. It works far more often than the best programs anyone can think up."

"Same salary? Five a week and expenses?"

"I ... well, okay. I can get by with that for a little while."

"You're on the clock as of now. Let me talk with our operative."

Phil handed Nort the phone.

What was that ... oh, shit! He ran into the house to find a big rat tranquilly eating the moldy bread on the kitchen counter. It had knocked a dish off onto the floor. He picked up a big knife and swung it at the rat. The rat dove off the counter and into the garbage pail. Phil slammed on the lid and took it outside.

He went back to tell Nort he would be getting to work right away. Nort asked if he should stay around.

"Why?"

He shrugged. Phil said it would be a lot better if he didn't have visitors from the department. They were too easy to spot. He'd be watched. If it looked like he didn't accept the job they'd get tired of it after a day or two.

Nort left. He went out to the rat – that had gnawed a hole in the plastic garbage pail and escaped.

He went inside and cleaned up the kitchen. Now that drain was stopped up, but he knew that was back-pressure from the earlier toilet episode, so used the plunger. He then went to his computer to work for awhile, finding every project he could.

  He then went to bed. Tomorrow would be something else! He wished he had a hint as to what.

One Year Later

Phil got out of bed and headed for the bathroom. He stepped into his slippers, one of which folded under. He almost fell, but caught the doorjamb. He cut himself slightly while he was shaving, then went into the kitchen to fix breakfast. He plugged in the coffee maker, which made a humming noise, then a pop.

He didn't pause. He took out a pan, dumped water in and coffee and sat it on the stove. He turned on the gas. There was a ball of fire that rose toward the ceiling a bit, then went out. Slow leak. He'd fixed it several times. He thought nothing of it. He rinsed the clean dishes in the drainer. He didn't doubt the rat had been in the house again. He wasn't about to take it outside if he got it again. It was a dead rat if he got it.

There was a knock on the door. He called that if they were there for God he'd see they got to him very fast. He'd told all of them not to come around anymore.

It was Gordon and Nort. They were going fishing. Did he want to come along? They were sort of pals. Gordon had confided after six months that he hadn't found two of the chickens. Both hens. It was long enough that the explosion thing was shown not to be passed on to any chicks and there hadn't been any exploding eggs they heard of. So long as no two of the chicks of those hens mated it was something in the past. Phil didn't try to explain skip-generation genetics. It probably wouldn't apply, anyhow.

"After last trip? When the trailer blew a tire, the motor never started, the plug came out and we almost sank? You would ask again?"

"It's really part of the job," Nort confided. "Don't let them know I told you that. They want to know how anyone can live with the constant crap your life is. It got to be a joke around the office. You came to the building twice and it almost burned down once and that bus went through the front door when the brakes failed the second time. They don't know how you can just go on like nothing happened."

"Oh, yeah. I hardly noticed. How is their program coming along?"

"Which one? You or the Flashlight Project?"

"That thing won't ever work. I gave them the facts about that. They ignored it. It wasn't what some bigshit scientist in Germany said. I showed them a few other things that ass said that were totally ridiculous.

"Come on in. Coffee should be ready."

He led them to the kitchen. They sat at the table. He got cups and a sock, strained the boiling coffee into the second pot, managed to spill some boiling water that barely missed going into his hand. When he pulled the hand away he managed to knock over the cooking oil that made a little puddle on the floor. He dropped some paper toweling on it and brought out the cream and sugar.

The cream was curdled. He dumped the glob into the sink and got some creamer in a jar. He turned to ask if they wanted some cinnamon rolls with the coffee, then banged his head on the cabinet door when he turned around again, not hard.

He poured his own cup and sat on the third chair. One leg collapsed, almost dumping him on the floor. He grabbed the fourth chair and sat in it, managing to dump over the creamer. Only a little spilled. Nort and Gordon were staring at him in disbelief. He didn't even seem to notice all the things that were happening.

He saw the looks. He grinned. "It's a little game God and I play. He tries to get a reaction, I refuse to react. It's just in fun ... I think."

He said there were some sticky buns in the other cabinet. He stood and opened the hanging cabinet door.

The rat jumped out almost into his face. He was finally fast enough to be able to swat it down. It was against the baseboard, scrambling to get to its feet. He smacked it with the frying pan. He got it by the tail and threw the lifeless body into the back yard.

"Pretty good one, Lord! I expected something such when I have guests. You'll have to get a new rat, I guess."

He washed his hands thoroughly and got the sticky buns. They were in a tin bread box, so the rat couldn't have gotten to them.

The three chatted awhile and ate the sticky buns. They still wanted to go fishing.

"Okay. We have a sort of agreement.

"Lord, how about a truce for the rest of the day? There's no reason for our little game to screw up the day for anyone else, like last time, okay? For now?"

He got a sort of agreement feeling, but knew things would go on happening, though they would only be things that didn't affect Nort and Gordon.

Like his reel with the wad of monofilament jamming it. Like the hooks on his favorite lure being rusted to where they would break if he got a big one. Like the smelly reel oil leaking all over the tackle box. Like the artificial worms leaking rancid liquid in the box. Like his beer cooler lid snapping in two.

He shook his head and dropped the tackle box into the trash can. He cut all the monofilament off the reel. They stopped at the shop where they launched the boat and Phil bought a lot of new stuff. What he'd made working for the government made it nothing.

"I see you bought stainless steel hooks this time," Nort noticed.

"I always do."

"But ... those were rusted you threw away!"

"Uh-huh. And?"

He shook his head. Phil slipped on the alga growing on the launch ramp, but caught onto the boat before he went down onto the concrete. His fishing hat blew off his head and got soaked.

Then they went out into the lake.

They were back at his house just before dark. He had a nice bass. He said there was always a consolation prize. He really did enjoy the game anymore.

He went into the kitchen when they left, still not quite believing the kinds of things that happened to Phil.

Phil managed to survive long enough to get to

bed. In the morning he went out to his coop – he really did build a small one for his own use – and got a dozen eggs. He put ten of them in the refrigerator and took a bowl to make a two egg omelet. He tapped the eggs to crack them. The second one exploded.

"Good show, Lord! You really got me on that one! A point up for you!

"Used the old skip-generation thing and I've got a hen that lays the eggs.? I'm glad they didn't have the acrylic part yet.

"You wouldn't do anything that really would seriously hurt me, would you?"

He cleaned up the mess.

Should he report this to the office?

No. It was a doomed trait. It would definitely be bred out of the chickens in the next generation.

Well! Things are normal! What should he do today?

C. D. Moulton's works are available on most major outlets as printed or e-books. CD writes the CD Grimes, PI mysteries, the Det. Lt. Nick Storie mysteries, the Clint Faraday mysteries, the Flight of the Maita science fiction series, books on orchid culture and many others of many types. Mystery, adventure, intrigue, science fiction, fantasy, paranormal, mild erotica, and factual.

www.ingramcontent.com/pod-product-compliance
Lightning Source LLC
Chambersburg PA
CBHW050603160726
48003CB00003B/1021